Love
is a
Stranger

Love
is a
Stranger

Selected Lyric Poetry of
Jelaluddin Rumi
Translated by Kabir Edmund Helminski

Threshold Books is committed to publishing books of spiritual signifi-
cance and high literary quality. All Threshold Books have sewn bindings
and are printed on acid-free paper. We will be happy to send you a catalog.

Threshold Books, RD 4 Box 600 Putney, Vermont 05346
Phone 802 254-8300 or 802 257-2779

Cover illustration from Isfahan, Persia, Seventeenth Century, courtesy of
the Sackler Gallery/Smithsonian Institute.

Jalal al-Din Rumi, Maulana, 1207-1273
Love is a stranger : selected lyric poetry of Jelaluddin Rumi /
translated by Kabir Edmund Helminski
96 p. 8.5"
ISBN 0-939660-32-6 : $9:00
1. Sufi poetry, Persian—Translations into English.
2. Sufi poetry, English—Translations from Persian.

I Helminski, Kabir Edmund 1947- .

Contents

Introduction

More than fourteen years have passed since I began to translate some of Rúmí's poetry. I could not have imagined where this path was taking me. What at first seemed a distant and exotic city in the distance, whose outline and features I was just beginning to differentiate, this city of Sufi verse, is now a more familiar place whose streets and alleys, whose grand architecture and precious details, I no longer view from afar but sense and feel as someone beginning to feel at home in a place. This world is as real and present to me as the outer world I live in, but even more so, for it is a world of meanings and not just things.

Western culture has no convenient category for Mevlána Jeláluddin Rúmí. In the Islamic world he is held in the highest esteem not only as a literary figure, but as a saint whose personal example inspired the founding of a major religious order, and as a philosopher whose elaboration of the cosmic sense of Love has had a significant cultural impact.

His literary genius is made clear in the 30,000 verses of impassioned lyric poetry in his *Diván-i Shamsi Tabriz* and in the 22,000 verses of his masterwork, the *Mathnáwí*, a vast tapestry into which has been woven Aesopian fables, scenes from the everyday life of his times, Qur'anic revelation, and Neoplatonic metaphysics. The great poet Abdur Rahmán Jámi called the *Mathnáwí* "the Qur'an in the Persian tongue." Sa'di, another major poet, once selected an ode of Mevlána's for presentation to the Moghul Khan as the best poem in the Persian language. In the West, Rúmí's influence has been felt by Chaucer, Goethe, and Emerson, to name

[5]

a few; and no less a critic than Doctor Johnson has said of him: "He makes plain to the Pilgrim the secrets of the Way of Unity, and unveils the Mysteries of the Path of Eternal Truth."

To many already familiar with his life and writings, Mevlána Jeláluddin Rúmí is something more than a poet. He might be considered an example of *insáni kámil,* the perfected or completed human being in whom the divine attributes are embodied. A figure of almost prophetic dimensions, he became for some Muslims almost a second Muhammad, for Christians a second Christ, and for Jews a second Moses. Among those present at his funeral procession were people of different religious traditions, each of whom claimed that Jeláluddin had brought him to a deeper understanding of his own faith.

Rúmí's work can be considered a synthesis of all that Islamic culture had assimilated from Arab, Hellenistic, Hermetic, Christian, Jewish, Persian, and Indian sources in the first seven hundred years of its existence. With complete respect for the prophets of the Judaeo-Christian-Islamic tradition and with uncommon beauty and insight, he elucidated the mythic inheritance, the shared traditions of his age; yet he was somehow beyond his own culture and time. Although following the details of the Islamic faith, Rúmí expounded a religion of Love. Without denying his own Islamic faith he was able to say, "The religion of Love is like no other," and "Gambling yourself away is beyond any religion."

For the Sufis, the gnostics of Islam, Love has always been a central theme. In Persia especially, the metaphor of Love, Lover, and Beloved was developed so vividly that its metaphoric significance was sometimes mistaken for wanton sensuality. The Andalusian philosopher-saint, Ibn ʿArabi, authored some of the most beautiful love poetry in the Arabic language at the same time that he developed one of the most comprehensive systems of metaphysics ever known. When compelled to defend his poetry against orthodox detractors, he was more than able to demonstrate that the language of love was an appropriate analog for spiritual realities. For Rúmí, especially, Love was the very cause of existence, the hand behind the puppets, the Grand Artificer.

When in middle age he met the vagabond saint, Shamsi Tabriz, Mevlána said, "The God which I have worshipped all my life appeared to me today in human form." This statement, however, should not be understood as the complete identification of the human and the divine. From the Islamic point of view no human being, not even the Prophet, could be identified with God. Nevertheless, for the Sufi mystic the phenomenal world is a bridge to the Real, and both Mevlána and Shams found in each other the most perfect example of the Friend. In each other's presence they were able to experience the unity of Love, Lover, and Beloved.

The meeting of Shams and Mevlána was like the conjunction of two great planets. They retired into a solitude which became legendary; but as in the conjunction of the sun and moon, the apparent darkness of eclipse was objectionable to some of Mevlána's former students. Jealousy arose and Shams departed suddenly, leaving Mevlána without the spiritual intimacy which they had enjoyed. Perhaps it was necessary that he experience the pain of separation in order to reach his own perfection. After some years Shams would return and meet his death at the hands of assassins, but not before Rúmí was completely transformed by his ardent love.

Mevlána would continue to discover the "Friend" in various guises through the rest of his life. After Shams it was Saláhuddin, a goldsmith who became a disciple, that Jelál would extol for his incomparable sanctity, and after Saláhuddin's death, Husamuddin, the recorder of the *Mathnáwi*. Characteristic of Rúmí's spirituality is the recognition of the Beloved or Friend in human form, not as the worship of personality, but as a recognition of the spiritual gifts the One continually bestows on His creatures. For Rúmí, as for many who have followed his way through the centuries, friendship and love are essential values. In the *Menáqibu al'Arifin*, Ahmed al- Afláki a disciple of the grandson of Rúmí, relates the following story on the subject of humility and respect:

> *Jelál spoke a parable from the trees of the field: "Every tree that yields no fruit, as the pine, the cypress, the box, etc., grows tall and straight, lifting its head up high, and sending all its branches upward; whereas all the fruit bearing trees droop their heads, and trail their branches."... In like manner, Jelál also had the commendable habit to show himself humble and considerate to all, even the lowest; especially so to children and old women. He used to bless them, and always bowed to them, even though these were not Muslims. Once he chanced upon a number of children who were playing, and who left their game, ran to him, and bowed, Jelál bowed to them also; so much so, that one little fellow called out from afar: "Wait for me until I come." Jelál did not move away, until the child had come, bowed, and been bowed to.*
>
> *At that time people were speaking and writing against him. Legal opinions were obtained and circulated, to the effect that music, singing, and dancing, are unlawful. Out of his kindly disposition and love of peace, Jelál made no reply: and after a while all his detractors were silenced, and their writings clean forgotten, as though they had never been written; whereas, his family and followers will endure to the end of time, and will go on increasing continually.*

The subject of Rúmí's poetry is not life but something altogether more than life. While most poetry leads us through carefully arranged thoughts and feelings, Rúmí writes from somewhere beyond thought and feeling as we know it: "Your thoughts are the bar behind the door! Set the wood on fire! Silence, heart!" His poetry is not so much the search for some immanent truth and knowledge, or some discovery to be made in the outer

[8]

world, but an elaboration of an instant *hereness*, the immediate inner song of experience that floods this world but is not of it. It is an ecstasy of knowledge that overflows into words, sounds, images. His is a knowledge of the Whole as well as the parts.

Rúmí is building a model of an immense inner world using every possible example and situation of the outer world as metaphor. The spiritual and poetic tradition that produced Rúmí, Sana'i, 'Attar, Sádi, and Jámi understands all of creation as providing the metaphors of Divine Qualities. Rúmí says that after seeing the face of one's Lord, the "whole earthly realm is fraud and fantasy." The Beloved, even when encountered in physical form, is just the exemplification of a spiritual Beloved entirely beyond form. If he mentions idols, he does not mean the literal idols of precious metals but the idols that are inwardly held, the representations of Reality that usurp the place of immediate perception. If he speaks of intoxication, he means the spiritual states which are a kind of sobriety compared to the intoxication of conventional life. Very little is what it appears to be. The Sufi poet inhabits many worlds simultaneously, "worlds within worlds," and therefore it is possible to speak of each line having at least seven levels of meaning, each corresponding to one of the seven heavens or worlds of Islamic cosmology.

While some poetry may attempt to break conventions of language and style, this poetry does more than that. It attempts to disturb conventions of thought and feeling, to peel back the skin of conditioning, to penetrate layers or expectation. Especially in the *Mathnáwi*, his method is to build on a theme with stories, images, ideas, and diversions, approaching the center from all points on the periphery, intending to elucidate what can only be called "the mysteries." Whether it is the melody of spiritual separation and solitude or the experience of connectedness and unity, it is sung with passion and immediacy. It is not an immediacy entirely absent from Western literatures, but this refinement of feeling is seldom found so unalloyed, so undiluted.

Rúmí's work is not the product of literary ambition, but an act of service. Most of his lyric poetry was spoken spontaneously and recorded by its hearers. Rumi did not make too much of his own poetry. He once said that just as a host must plunge his hands into the cleaning of tripe, because that is what his guest has an appetite for, so he occupied himself with poetry. Afláki, however, relates these words of Mevlána's concerning his verses:

> *The great Causer of all causes caused a source of affection to arise, and out of the wilderness of causelessness raised a means by which I was attracted from the land of Khorasan to the land of the Romans (Asia Minor). That country he made a home for my children and posterity, in order that, with the elixir of grace, the copper of their existences might be transmuted into gold and into philosopher-stone, they themselves being received into the communion of saints. When I perceived that they had no inclination for the practice of religious austerities, and no knowledge of the divine mysteries, I imagined to arrange metrical exhortations and musical services, as being captivating for men's minds, and especially so for the Romans, who are naturally of a lively disposition and fond of incisive expositions. Even as a sick child is coaxed into taking a salutary, though nauseous medicine, in like manner, were the Romans led by art to acquire a taste for spiritual truth.*

Although Rúmí was one of the first of the major Persian poets to receive the attention of the West and numerous translations have been completed, it has been about seventy years since the publication of the English translations on which we depend. With all respect for James Redhouse, the great R.A. Nicholson, and his student, A.J. Arberry, what they gave us in English were accurate word for word versions in Victorian prose. Even Arberry, the most recent of the three has confessed: "These versions, being in the vast majority the first renderings into a Western language, and intended primarily for nonspecialists, have been made as literal as possible, with a minimum concession to readability."

We have also seen "versions" of Rumi's work, i.e. renderings that use a literal translation of the text as a starting point for a poet to recreate a poem based on the original. Coleman Barks and Robert Bly, among others, have worked in this way, not only with Rúmí, but with other spiritual writers as well. Some of these versions have been very successful as poetry and have been helpful in introducing Rúmí to the modern world. It deserves to be mentioned, however, that versions, whatever their value, grant more license to the personal voice and imagination of the writer creating the versions.

The problem of translating Rúmí has two aspects that I would like to mention. First, the translator must not only acquaint himself with the cultural background of the work but should have some affinity or experience with the esoteric traditions out of which the poetry grew. Secondly, he must find or create equivalent terms for experiences that might themselves be almost anachronistic to the modern mentality. I agree with the poet and critic Kathleen Raine who has said that the work of any serious artist or poet in our time is "to recreate a common language for the communication of knowledge of spiritual realities, and of the invisible order of the psyche."

From the beginning my intention has been to present accurate translations of the texts as poetry in contemporary English. English is much closer to Persian, an essentially Indo-European tongue, than it is, say, to Arabic or Turkish. Rumi's lines have an elegant simplicity about them which is best translated, it seems to me, by mostly anglo-saxon words usually of one or two syllables, rather than by longer words from a more Latinate vocabulary. Furthermore, the meter and rhymes of Persian would become tedious in English and have not been reproduced, although in some cases meter and assonance have been used. English has its own possibilities for meaning and music, and it is necessary to work within these possibilities while being faithful to the tone and spirit of the original. Rúmí's language is sublime, yet without affectation or formality; and even in his most intoxicated verses he expresses a refinement and dignity.

The first half of *Love is a Stranger* includes work that has been translated since the publication of *Ruins of the Heart* in 1980; the second half contains most of *Ruins of the Heart*, although in a slightly revised form. In some cases I have taken the liberty of breaking the lines differently than the originals. I have also taken the liberty of giving titles to these selections, although they originally had none. It is a liberty which I will justify by saying that a title can sometimes help us to identify and recall particular poems.

I wish to thank the people who have encouraged this work, and especially Marzieh Gail who first guided my study of the Persian language, led me line by line through the beauty of Mevlána's work, and without whom I could not have attempted these translations. I would also like to express my deep gratitude to the late Shaikh Suleyman Hayati Dede of the Mevlevi Order, successor to Mevlána Jeláluddin Rúmí, whose kind example and understanding brought me closer to a living experience and taste of the essence of Mevlána's life.

Kabir Helminski

Love
is a
Stranger

The Ruby

At breakfast tea a beloved asked her lover,
"Who do you love more, yourself or me?"

"From my head to my foot I have become you.
Nothing remains of me but my name.
You have your wish. Only you exist.
I've disappeared like a drop of vinegar
in an ocean of honey."

A stone which has become a ruby
is filled with the qualities of the sun.
No stoniness remains in it.
If it loves itself, it is loving the sun.
And if it loves the sun, it is loving itself.
There is no difference between these two loves.

Before the stone becomes the ruby, it is its own enemy.
Not one but two exist.
The stone is dark and blind to daylight.
If it loves itself, it is unfaithful: it intensely resists the sun.
If it says "I," it is all darkness.
A pharoah claims divinity and is brought down.
Hallaj says the same and is saved.
One I is cursed, another I is blessed.
One I is a stone, another a crystal.
One an enemy of the light, the other a reflector of it.
In its inmost consciousness, not through any doctrine,
it is one with the light.

Work on your stony qualities
and become resplendent like the ruby.
Practice self-denial and accept difficulty.
Always see infinite life in letting the self die.
Your stoniness will decrease; your ruby nature will grow.
The signs of self-existence will leave your body,
and ecstasy will take you over.

Become all hearing like an ear and gain a ruby earring.
Dig a well in the earth of this body,
or even before the well is dug,
let God draw the water up.

Be always at work scraping the dirt from the well.
To everyone who suffers,
perseverance brings good fortune.
The Prophet has said that each prostration of prayer
is a knock on heaven's door.
When anyone continues to knock,
felicity shows its smiling face.

The Root of the Root of Your Self

Don't go away, come near.
Don't be faithless, be faithful.
Find the antidote in the venom.
Come to the root of the root of yourself.

Molded of clay, yet kneaded
from the substance of certainty,
a guard at the Treasury of Holy Light—
come, return to the root of the root of your Self.

Once you get hold of selflessness,
you'll be dragged from your ego
and freed from many traps.
Come, return to the root of the root of your Self.

You are born from the children of God's creation,
but you have fixed your sight too low.
How can you be happy?
Come, return to the root of the root of your Self.

Although you are a talisman protecting a treasure,
you are also the mine.
Open your hidden eyes
and come to the root of the root of your Self.

You were born from a ray of God's majesty
and have the blessings of a good star.

Why suffer at the hands of things that don't exist?
Come, return to the root of the root of your Self.

You are a ruby embedded in granite.
How long will you pretend it isn't true?
We can see it in your eyes.
Come to the root of the root of your Self.

You came here from the presence of that fine Friend,
a little drunk, but gentle, stealing our hearts
with that look so full of fire; so,
come, return to the root of the root of your Self.

Our master and host, Shamsi Tabrizi,
has put the eternal cup before you.
Glory be to God, what a rare wine!
So come, return to the root of the root of your Self.

Love is a Stranger

*H*eart came on solid footing with breath refined
to warn the best of communities.
Heart placed your head
like a pen on the page of love.

We are joyous pennants in your just wind.
Master, to where do you dance?

Toward the land of liberation,
toward the plain of non-existence.

Master, tell us which non-existence you mean.
The ear of eternity knows the letter of eternity.

Love is a stranger with a strange language,
like an Arab in Persia. I have brought a story;
it is strange, like the one who tells it.
Listen to your servant.

Joseph's face enlightened the well in which he was suspended
His imprisonment became a palace
with orchards and meadows, a paradise,
a royal hall, and a chamber of sanctity.

Just as you toss a stone into the water,
the water at that very moment parts to receive it.
Just as a cloudy night is dispelled by a clear dawn,
from his humiliation and loss he views high heaven.

Reason, do not envy my mouth.
God witnesses the blessings.
Though the tree drinks from hidden roots,
we see the display of its branches.
Whatever the earth took from heaven,
it yields up honestly in spring.

Whether you have stolen a bead or a jewel,
whether you have raised a flag or a pen,
the night is gone and day has arrived,
and the sleeper shall see what he has dreamed.

A New Rule

It is the rule with drunkards to fall upon each other,
to quarrel, become violent, and make a scene.
The lover is even worse than a drunkard.
I will tell you what love is: to enter a mine of gold.
And what is that gold?

The lover is a king above all kings,
unafraid of death, not at all interested in a golden crown.
The dervish has a pearl concealed under his patched cloak.
Why should he go begging door to door?

Last night that moon came along,
drunk, dropping clothes in the street.
"Get up," I told my heart, "Give the soul a glass of wine.
The moment has come to join the nightingale in the garden,
to taste sugar with the soul-parrot."

I have fallen, with my heart shattered—
where else but on your path? And I
broke your bowl, drunk, my idol, so drunk,
don't let me be harmed, take my hand.

A new rule, a new law has been born:
break all the glasses and fall toward the glassblower.

The Intellectual

The intellectual is always showing off;
the lover is always getting lost.
The intellectual runs away, afraid of drowning;
the whole business of love is to drown in the sea.
Intellectuals plan their repose;
lovers are ashamed to rest.
The lover is always alone, even surrounded with people;
like water and oil, he remains apart.
The man who goes to the trouble
of giving advice to a lover
get's nothing. He's mocked by passion.
Love is like musk. It attracts attention.
Love is a tree, and lovers are its shade.

Didn't I Say?

Didn't I say, "Don't go there; I am your friend.
In this mirage of existence, I am the fountain of life."
Even if your anger takes you a hundred thousand years away,
in the end you will return, for I am your goal.
Didn't I say, "Don't be content with earthly forms;
I am the designer of the intimate chamber of your contentment."
Didn't I say, "I am the sea, and you are a single fish;
don't strand yourself on dry land; I am your clear sea."
Didn't I say, "Don't get caught in the trap like a helpless bird;
I am the power of flight—your feet and your wings."
Didn't I say, "They will waylay you and make you cold;
I am the fire and your warm desire."
Didn't I say, "They will implant their qualities in you
until you forget that the best qualities are here."
Didn't I say, "You do not know from what direction
your affairs are put in order."
I am the Creator beyond directions.
If light is in your heart, find your way home.
If you are of God, know your Benefactor.

On the Deathbed

Go, rest your head on a pillow, leave me alone;
leave me ruined, exhausted from the journey of this night,
writhing in a wave of passion till the dawn.
Either stay and be forgiving,
or, if you like, be cruel and leave.
Flee from me, away from trouble;
take the path of safety, far from this danger.
We have crept into this corner of grief,
turning the water wheel with a flow of tears.
While a tyrant with a heart of flint slays,
and no one says, "Prepare to pay the blood money."
Faith in the king comes easily in lovely times,
but be faithful now and endure, pale lover.
No cure exists for this pain but to die,
so why should I say, "Cure this pain"?
In a dream last night I saw
an ancient one in the garden of love,
beckoning with his hand, saying, "Come here."
On this path, Love is the emerald,
the beautiful green that wards off dragons.
Enough, I am losing myself.
If you are a man of learning,
read something classic,
a history of the human struggle
and don't settle for mediocre verse.

A House for the Naked

It's late and it's raining, my friends;
let's go home. Let's leave these ruins
we've haunted like owls.
Even though these blonde beauties beckon,
let's go home. All the reasons offered
by the sensible, dull, and sorrowful
can't darken our hearts now;
nor can all this phantom love play,
this imaginary paradise hold us back.
Some see the grain but not the harvest.
Don't ask too many "how's" or "why's."
Let beasts graze.
Come home to the real celebration and music.
Shams has built a house for the naked and the pure.

Like Sunlight Upon the Earth

I am from you, and at the same time, you have devoured me.
I melt in you since through you I froze.
You squeeze me with your hand,
and then you step on me with your foot.
This is how the grape becomes wine.
You cast us like sunlight upon the earth.
And our light, passing through the body
as if it were an open window to our Source,
returns, purified, to You.
Whoever sees that sun says,
"He is alive,"
and whoever sees only the window says,
"He is dying."
He has veiled our origin in that cup of pain and joy.
Within our core we are pure;
all the rest is dregs.
Source of the soul of souls, Shams, the Truth of Tabriz,
a hundred hearts are afire for you.

The War Inside

Rest your cheek, for a moment,
on this drunken cheek.
Let me forget the war and cruelty inside myself.
I hold these silver coins in my hand;
give me Your wine of golden light.
You have opened the seven doors of heaven;
now lay Your hand generously on my tightened heart.
All I have to offer is this illusion, my self.
Give it a nickname at least that is real.
Only you can restore what You have broken;
help my broken head.
I'm not asking for some sweet pistachio candy,
but Your everlasting love.
Fifty times I've said,
"Heart, stop hunting and step into this net."

Buy Me From My Words

Before now I wanted
to be paid for what I said,
but now I need you
to buy me from my words.
The idols I used to carve
charmed everyone. Now I'm drunk
on Abraham and tired of idols.
An idol with no color or scent
ended my whole career.
Find someone else for the job.
A happy madman without a thought,
I have swept the shop clean.
If something enters my mind,
I say, "Leave. You're a distraction."
Whatever is coarse and heavy, I destroy.
Who should be with Layla?
Someone who can be Majnun.
The man holding up this waving flag
actually belongs to the other side.

What a Man Can Say

In the name of friendship,
don't repeat to my Beloved
all that I said last night,
out of my mind;
but if, by God, she hears it,
she'll understand what a man can say
in the dark, loud or quiet, rough or soft,
when reason is not at home.
If God let's this anxiety out,
no one in the world will stay sane.
Mind, are these your dark suggestions?
Cloud, is this your sad rain?
Believers, watch your hearts.
Curious or kind, stay away.

This Marriage

May these vows and this marriage be blessed.
May it be sweet milk,
this marriage, like wine and halvah.
May this marriage offer fruit and shade
like the date palm.
May this marriage be full of laughter,
our every day a day in paradise.
May this marriage be a sign of compassion,
a seal of happiness here and hereafter.
May this marriage have a fair face and a good name,
an omen as welcome
as the moon in a clear blue sky.
I am out of words to describe
how spirit mingles in this marriage.

Clothes Abandoned on the Shore

Your body is here with us,
but your heart is in the meadow.
You travel with the hunters
though you yourself are what they hunt.

Like a reed flute,
you are encased by your body,
with a restless breathy sound inside.

You are a diver;
your body is just clothing left at the shore.
You are a fish whose way is through water.

In this sea there are many bright veins
and some that are dark.
The heart receives its light
from those bright veins.

If you lift your wing
I can show them to you.
You are hidden like the blood within,
and you are shy to the touch.

Those same veins sing a melancholy tune
in the sweet-stringed lute,
music from a shoreless sea
whose waves roar out of infinity.

The Pull of Love

When Hallaj found union with his Beloved,
it was right that it was on the gallows.

I snatched a cap's worth of cloth from his coat,
and it covered my reason, my head, and my feet.

I pulled a thorn from the fence of his garden,
and it has not stopped working its way into my heart.

One morning a little of his wine
turned my heart into a lion hunter.
It's right that this separation he helped me feel
lurks like a monster within my heart.

Yet heaven's wild and unbroken colt
was trained by the hand of his love.
Though reason is learned and has its honors,
it pawned its cap and robes for a cup of love.

Many hearts have sought refuge from this love,
but it drags and pulls them to its own refuge.

One cold day a bearskin was floating down the river.
I said to a man who had no clothes,
"Jump in and pull it out."

But the bearskin was a live bear,
and the man who jumped in so eagerly

was caught in the clutches of what he went to grab.

"Let go of it," I said, "Fighting won't get you anywhere."
"Let go of it? This coat won't let go of me!"
Silence. Just a hint. Who needs volumes of stories?

Sweep the Dust off the Sea

The Beautiful One handed me a broom and said,
"Sweep the dust from the sea!",

then burned the broom in the fireplace and said,
"Give me back my broom."

Bewildered, I put my head to the ground.
"In real submission there's no longer
even someone to bow."

"But how?"
"Without hesitation or anything of yourself."

I bared my neck and said,
"Sever me from myself with Ali's sword."

But as I was struck, and struck again,
countless heads appeared.

As if I were a lamp, and each head a wick,
flames rose on every side,

countless candle-eyed heads,
a procession spanning East and West.
But what is East or West within placelessness?

It's all a furnace and a bath house.

[33]

Your heart is cool; how long will you lie in this
warm bath house?

Leave the bath house and its stove.
Undress yourself in the inner world
and appreciate the frescoes, the beautiful figures,
colored with the hues of the tulip bed;
look towards the window that lets in the light.

The six directions are the bath house,
and a window opens toward the placeless.
Above it is the beauty of a Sovereign

from whose reflection the earth and the sky
received their color, from Whom soulfulness
has rained down upon the Turk and Zanzibari.

The day is gone, and my story ends.
Night and day are shamed by my beauty's story.

The Sun of Tabriz keeps me
drunk and languishing in this state.

And He is With Us

Totally unexpected my guest arrived.
"Who is it?" asked my heart.
"The face of the moon," said my soul.

As he entered the house,
we all ran into the street madly looking for the moon.
"I'm in here," he was calling from inside,
but we were calling him outside unaware of his call.
Our drunken nightingale is singing in the garden,
and we are cooing like doves, "Where, where, where?"

A crowd formed: "Where's the thief?"
And the thief among us is saying,
"Yeah, where's the thief."
All our voices became mixed together
and not one voice stood out from the others.

And He is with you means He is searching with you.
He is nearer to you than yourself. Why look outside?
Become like melting snow; wash yourself of yourself.
With love your inner voice will find a tongue
 growing like a silent white lily in the heart.

You and I

A moment of happiness,
you and I sitting on the verandah,
apparently two, but one in soul, you and I.

We feel the flowing water of life here,
you and I, with the garden's beauty and the birds singing.
The stars will be watching us,
and we will show them
what it means to be a thin crescent moon.

You and I unselfed, will be together,
indifferent to idle speculation, you and I.
The parrots of heaven will be cracking sugar
as we laugh together, you and I.

And what is even more amazing
is that while here together, you and I
are at this very moment in Iraq and Khorasan.
In one form upon this earth,
and in another form in a timeless sweet land.

Search the Darkness

Sit with your friends; don't go back to sleep.
Don't sink like a fish to the bottom of the sea.

Surge like an ocean,
don't scatter yourself like a storm.

Life's waters flow from darkness.
Search the darkness, don't run from it.

Night travelers are full of light,
and you are, too; don't leave this companionship.

Be a wakeful candle in a golden dish,
don't slip into the dirt like quicksilver.

The moon appears for night travelers,
be watchful when the moon is full.

The Ninth Month

You watch the sensuous movements of the veil.
Do you know there's a Chinese girl behind it
whose face you can't see?

You see a reflection of the real moon
in all the stones that lie at your feet.

You're a leaf scattered by an invisible wind.
Don't you know something's moving you?

Unless some thought stirs that wind, you don't stir.
If the wind isn't still, you're not.

Constellations, planets, your inmost states
are like camels in a row. You're the last.

Curl up and drink in the blood
like a child in heaven's womb.

You feel a pain in the sphere of your heart,
but when you lift your head it's gone.

Your ninth month is Shams' face,
you, who have been trusted with the secret of both worlds.

O heart, be patient in this blood
until the ninth month.

This Useless Heart

Heart, since you embraced the mysteries,
you have become useless for anything else.
Go mad, don't stay sane.
People meditate to get something.
All you do is give.
Crazy Majnun's priorities are now yours, too.

If you want to be respectable,
why do you go downtown drunk?
It's no good just sitting in some corner,
once you've made friends with the dissolute of this path.

Go back to the desert;
leave this shabby town.
There's the smell of a tavern
somewhere in this neighborhood,
and it's already got you high.

Now follow it. Go to Qaf Mountain like the Simurgh,
leave these owls and herons.
Go into the thicket of Reality like a lion.
Why linger with hyenas and dogs?
Don't go after the scent of Joseph's shirt,
you are already mourning his death like Jacob, his father.

Expansion and Contraction

Before everything you own slips away,
tell the material world, like Mary:
My refuge is with the Merciful.

In her room Mary had seen something
that won her heart, something intensely alive.
That trusted spirit rose from the face of the earth
like a sun or moon rising in the East,
like beauty unveiled.

Mary, who was undressed, began to tremble,
afraid of the evil that might be in it.
This kind of thing could cause
Joseph to cut his own wrist.
It flowered in front of her like a rose,
like a fantasy that lifts its head in the heart.

Mary became selfless and in this selflessness
she said, "I will leap into God's protection,"
because that pure bosomed one
could take herself to the Unseen.
Since she thought this world a temporary kingdom,
she built her fortress in Presence,
so that in the hour of death
she would be invulnerable.

She saw no better protection than God;
she made her home near to His castle.

[40]

Those glances of love were arrows,
piercing and killing all reason.
The army and its leaders are enthralled by Him.
Those with wit are made witless by Him.
Hundreds of thousands of kings are in His service.
Hundreds of thousands of full moons
are dedicated to the all night fever of His love.
Zuhra cannot breathe a word;
universal reason, on seeing Him, is humbled.

What shall I say? He has sealed my lips.
The channel of my breath is hooked up to His furnace.
"I am the smoke of that fire, the evidence of it."
The only evidence for the sun is its towering light.
What shadow could claim to be that evidence?
It is enough for the shadow to submit itself before Him.
The majesty of this evidence declares the truth.

He is ahead, and all perceptions must fall behind.
All perceptions are riding on lame donkeys,
while He is an arrow travelling through space.
If He chooses to escape,
none can even find the dust He leaves behind;
and if they choose to flee, He simply bars the way.

Every perception is disquieting:
this is the moment for struggle, not for lifting the goblet.
One bird of perception is soaring like a falcon,

another is tearing through the air like an arrow,
another is out sailing like a ship,
and another is constantly turning back.

When something to chase appears in the distance,
all these birds speed towards it,
but when it disappears, they are lost.
Like owls they return to the wilderness,
waiting, with one eye open and one eye closed,
for some prey to appear.
If they have to wait too long, they wonder,
was it something real or not?

The best course would be to rest a while
and gather some strength and vigor.
If night never came, people would waste themselves
pursuing all that they desire.
They would give their own bodies to be consumed
for the sake of their desire and greed,
but night appears, a treasure of Mercy,
to save them from desires for a short while.

When you feel contraction, traveler,
it's for your own good. Don't burn with grief.
In the state of expansion and delight
you are spending something, and that spending
needs the income of pain.

If it were always summertime,
the blazing heat would burn the garden,

soil and roots, so that nothing would ever grow again.
December is grim yet kind;
summer is all laughter, and yet it burns.

When contraction comes, see the expansion in it;
be cheerful, don't frown.
The children laugh; the sages look serious.
Sorrow is from the liver and laughter from the lungs.
The eyes of a child, like those of an ass,
are fixed only on its stall;
while the eyes of the wise see to the end.

Mathnawi III, 3700-3741

The Guest House

Darling, the body is a guest house;
every morning someone new arrives.
Don't say, "O, another weight around my neck!"
or your guest will fly back to nothingness.
Whatever enters your heart is a guest
from the invisible world: entertain it well.

Every day, and every moment a thought comes
like an honored guest into your heart.
My soul, regard each thought as a person,
for every person's value is in the thought they hold.

If a sorrowful thought stands in the way,
it is also preparing the way for joy.
It furiously sweeps your house clean
in order that some new joy may appear from the Source.
It scatters the withered leaves from the bough of the heart,
in order that fresh green leaves might grow.
It uproots the old joy so that
a new joy may enter from Beyond.

Sorrow pulls up the rotten root
that was veiled from sight.
Whatever sorrow takes away or causes the heart to shed,
it puts something better in its place—
especially for one who is certain
that sorrow is the servant of the intuitive.

Without the frown of clouds and lightning,
the vines would be burned by the smiling sun.
Both good and bad luck become guests in your heart:
like planets traveling from sign to sign.
When something transits your sign, adapt yourself,
and be as harmonious as its ruling sign,
so that when it rejoins the Moon,
it will speak kindly to the Lord of the heart.

Whenever sorrows come again,
meet it with smiles and laughter,
saying, "O my Creator, save me from its harm:
and do not deprive me of its good.
Lord, remind me to be thankful,
let me feel no regret if its benefit passes away.

And if the pearl is not in sorrow's hand,
let it go and still be pleased.
Increase your sweet practice.
Your practice will benefit you at another time;
someday your need will be suddenly fulfilled.

Mathnawi V: 3644-6; 3676-88; 3693-6; 3700-1.

The Ruins of the Heart

The Ruins of the Heart

I am a sculptor, a molder of form.
In every moment I shape an idol.
But then, in front of you, I melt them down.

I can rouse a hundred forms and fill them with spirit,
but when I look into your face,
I want to throw them in the fire.

Do you merely fill this drunkard's glass,
or do you really oppose the sober?
Is it you who brings to ruin
every house I build?

My soul spills into yours and is blended.
Because my soul has absorbed your fragrance,
I cherish it.

Every drop of blood I spill
informs the earth
I merge with my Beloved when I participate in love.

In this house of mud and water,
my heart has fallen into ruins.
Enter this house, my Love, or let me leave.

Song of the Reed

Listen to the reed and the tale it tells,
how it sings of separation:
Ever since they cut me from the reed bed,
my wail has caused men and women to weep.
I want a heart torn open with longing
to share the pain of this love.
Whoever has been parted from his source
longs to return to that state of union.
At every gathering I play my lament.
I'm a friend to both happy and sad.
Each befriended me for his own reasons,
yet none searched out the secrets I contain.
My secret is not different than my lament,
yet this is not for the senses to perceive.
The body is not hidden from the soul,
nor is the soul hidden from the body,
and yet the soul is not for everyone to see.
This flute is played with fire, not with wind,
and without this fire you would not exist.
It is the fire of love that inspires the flute.
It is the ferment of love that completes the wine.
The reed is a comfort to all estranged lovers.
Its music tears our veils away. Have you
ever seen a poison or antidote like the reed?
Have you seen a more intimate companion and lover?
It sings of the path of blood;
it relates the passion of Majnun.

Only to the senseless is this sense confided.
Does the tongue have any patron but the ear?
Our days grow more unseasonable,
these days which mix with grief and pain. . .
but if the days that remain are few,
let them go; it doesn't matter. But You, You remain,
for nothing is as pure as You are.
All but the fish quickly have their fill of His water;
and the day is long without His daily bread.

Break your bonds, be free, my child!
How long will silver and gold enslave you?
If you pour the whole sea into a jug,
will it hold more than one day's store?
The greedy eye, like the jug, is never filled.
Until content, the oyster holds no pearl.
Only one who has been undressed by Love
is free of defect and desire.
O Gladness, O Love, our partner in trade,
healer of all our ills, our Plato and Galen,
remedy of our pride and our vanity.
With love this earthly body could soar in the air;
the mountain could arise and nimbly dance.
Love gave life to Mount Sinai, O lover.
Sinai was drunk; Moses lost consciousness.
Pressed to the lips of one in harmony with myself,
I might also tell all that can be told;

[51]

but without a common tongue, I am dumb,
even if I have a hundred songs to sing.
When the rose is gone and the garden faded,
you will no longer hear the nightingale's song.
The Beloved is all; the lover just a veil.
The Beloved is living; the lover a dead thing.
If Love witholds its strengthening care,
the lover is left like a bird without wings.
How will I be awake and aware
if the light of the Beloved is absent?
Love wills that this Word be brought forth.
If you find the mirror of the heart dull,
the rust has not been cleared from its face.
O friends, listen to this tale,
the marrow of our inward state.

Mathnawi, I, I-35

Love is Reckless

Love is reckless; not reason.
Reason seeks a profit.
Love comes on strong, consuming herself, unabashed.

Yet, in the midst of suffering,
Love proceeds like a millstone,
hard surfaced and straightforward.

Having died to self-interest,
she risks everything and asks for nothing.
Love gambles away every gift God bestows.

Without cause God gave us Being;
without cause, give it back again.
Gambling yourself away is beyond any religion.

Religion seeks grace and favor,
but those who gamble these away are God's favorites,
for they neither put God to the test
nor knock at the door of gain and loss.

Mathnawi, VI, 1967-1974

When a Man and a Woman Become One

I darkened my eyes
with the dust of sadness
until each of them was a sea full of pearls.

All the tears which we creatures shed for Him
are not tears as many think but pearls. . . .

I am complaining about the Soul of the soul,
but I'm no complainer; I'm simply saying how it is.

My heart tells me it is distressed with Him,
but I can only laugh at such pretended injuries.

Be fair, You who are the Glory of the just.
You, Soul, free of "we" and "I,"
subtle spirit within each man and woman.

When a man and a woman become one,
that "one" is You.
And when that one is obliterated, there You are.

Where is this "we" and this "I"?
By the side of the Beloved.
You made this "we" and this "I"
in order that you might play

this game of courtship with Yourself,
that all "you's" and "I's" might become one soul
and finally drown in the Beloved.

All this is true. Come!
You who are the Creative Word: *Be*.
You, so far beyond description.

Is it possible for the bodily eye to see You?
Can thought comprehend Your laughter or grief?
Tell me now, can it possibly see You at all?
Such a heart has only borrowed things to live with.

The garden of love is green without limit
and yields many fruits other than sorrow or joy.
Love is beyond either condition:
without spring, without autumn, it is always fresh.

Mathnawi, I, 1779-1794

I Am Not. . . .

What shall I do, O Muslims?
I do not recognize myself. . . .
I am neither Christian nor Jew,
nor Magian, nor Muslim.
I am not of the East, nor the West,
not of the land, nor the sea.
I am not from nature's mine,
nor from the circling stars.
I am neither of earth nor water,
neither of wind nor fire.
I am not of the empyrean,
nor of the dust on this carpet.
I am not of the deep, nor from behind.
I am not of India or China,
not of Bulgaria, nor Saqsin;
I am not of the kingdom of Iraqain,
nor of the land of Khorasan.
I am not of this world nor the next,
not of heaven, nor of purgatory.
My place is the placeless,
my trace is the traceless.
It is not the body nor is it the soul,
for I belong to the soul of my love.
I have put duality away
and seen the two worlds as one.
One I seek, One I know.
One I see, One I call.

He is the First, He is the Last.
He is the Outward, He is the Inward.
I know of nothing but *Hu*, none but him.
Intoxicated with the cup of Love,
two worlds slip from my hands.
I am occupied with nothing
but fun and carousing.
If once in my life I pass a moment without You,
I repent my life from that moment on.
If once in this world
I should win a moment with You,
I will put both worlds under my feet
and dance forever in joy.
O Shams of Tabriz, I am so drunk in the world
that except for revelry and intoxication
I have no tale to tell.

When Names Did Not Exist

On that day when names did not exist,
nor any sign of anything to name: *I was.*
Things and their names came from me,
but that day was before "me" or "us."
A wisp of Love's hair was given as a sign,
and yet that wisp of hair was not.
Cross and Christians end to end,
but Love was not yet upon the cross.
At the house of idols, at the ancient temple,
not a trace was to be seen.
To the mountains I went—Herat and Kandahar—
and saw nothing above or below.
I climbed the summit of Mount Qaf
and found only the Simurgh there.
The reins of my search led me to the Kaaba,
but Love was not at the goal of old and young.
I asked Ibn Sinna in his ecstasy,
but it was not within his extent.
I was "within two bow-lengths"
and found nothing in that high court.
I paid attention to my heart—
and that was the place, nowhere else.
Except for Shamsi Tabriz, that pure spirit,
no one ever was intoxicated, distraught, and in love.

To Take a Step Without Feet

This is love: to fly toward a secret sky,
to cause a hundred veils to fall each moment.
First, to let go of life.
In the end, to take a step without feet;
to regard this world as invisible,
and to disregard what appears to the self.

Heart, I said, what a gift it has been
to enter this circle of lovers,
to see beyond seeing itself,
to reach and feel within the breast.

My soul, where does this breathing arise?
How does this beating heart exist?
Bird of the soul, speak in your own words,
and I will understand.

The heart replied: I was in the workplace
the day this house of water and clay was fired.
I was already fleeing that created house,
even as it was being created.
When I could no longer resist, I was dragged down,
and my features were molded from a handful of earth.

The Man of God

The man of God is drunken while sober.
The man of God is full without meat.
The man of God is perplexed and bewildered.
The man of God neither sleeps nor eats.
The man of God is a king clothed in rags.
The man of God is a treasure in the streets.
The man of God is neither of sky nor land.
The man of God is neither of earth nor sea.
The man of God is an ocean without end.
The man of God drops pearls at your feet.
The man of God has a hundred moons at night.
The man of God has a hundred suns' light.
The man of God's knowledge is complete.
The man of God doesn't read with his sight.
The man of God is beyond form and disbelief.
The man of God sees good and bad alike.
The man of God is far beyond non-being.
The man of God is seen riding high.
The man of God is hidden, Shamsuddin.
The man of God you must seek and find.

A World with no Boundaries

With every breath the sound
of love surrounds us,
and we are bound for the depths
of space, without distraction.

We've been in orbit before
and know the angels there.
Let's go there again, Master,
for that is our land.

Yet we are beyond all of that
and more than angels.
Out beyond duality,
we have a home, and it is Majesty.
That pure substance is
different from this dusty world.
What kind of place is this?
We once came down; soon we'll return.
A new happiness befriends us
as we work at offering our lives.

Muhammad, the jewel of the world,
is our caravan's chosen guide.
The sweetness we breathe on the wind
is from the scent of his hair,
and the radiance of our thought
is from the light of his day.

His face once caused
the moon to split in two.
She couldn't endure the sight of him.
Yet how lucky she was,
she who humbly received him.
Look into your heart and see
the splitting moon within each breath.
Having seen that vision,
how can you still dream?

When the wave of *Am I not?* struck,
it wrecked the body's ship;
when the ship wrecks again,
it will be the time of union.

The Human Being, like a bird of the sea,
emerged from the ocean of the soul.
Earth is not the final place of rest
for a bird born from the sea.

No, we are pearls of that ocean;
all of us live in it;
and if it weren't so, why would
wave upon wave arrive?

This is the time of union,
the time of eternal beauty.
It is the time of luck and kindness;
it is the ocean of purity.
The wave of bestowal has come.

The roar of the sea is here.
The morning of happiness has dawned.
No, it is the light of God.

Whose face is pictured here?
Who is this shah or prince?
Who is this ancient intelligence?
They are all masks . . .
and the only remedy is
this boiling ecstasy of the soul.

A fountain of refreshment
is in the head and the eyes —
not this bodily head
but another pure, spiritual one.

Many a pure head has been spilled
in the dust. Know the one from the other!
Our original head is hidden,
while this other is visible.
Beyond this world is a world
that has no boundaries.

Put your water skin away, brother,
and draw some wine from our cask!
The clay jug of perception
has such a narrow spout.
The sun appeared from the direction of Tabriz,
and I said, "This light is at once joined
with all things, and yet apart from everything."

Be Lost in the Call

Lord, said David, since you do not need us,
why did you create these two worlds?

Reality replied: O prisoner of time,
I was a secret treasure of kindness and generosity,
and I wished this treasure to be known,
so I created a mirror: it's shining face, the heart;
it's darkened back, the world;
The back would please you if you've never seen the face.

Has anyone ever produced a mirror out of mud and straw?
Yet clean away the mud and straw,
and a mirror might be revealed.

Until the juice ferments a while in the cask,
it isn't wine. If you wish your heart to be bright,
you must do a little work.

My King addressed the soul of my flesh:
You return just as you left.
Where are the traces of my gifts?

We know that alchemy transforms copper into gold.
This Sun doesn't want a crown or a robe from God's grace.
He is a hat to a hundred bald men,
a covering for ten who were naked.

Jesus sat humbly on the back of an ass, my child!
How could a zephyr ride an ass?
Spirit, find your way, in seeking lowness like a stream.
Reason, tread the path of selflessness into eternity.

Remember God so much that you are forgotten.
Let the caller and the called disappear;
be lost in the Call.

The House of Love

Why is there always music in this house?
Ask the owner.

Idols inside the Kaaba?
God's light in a pagan temple?

Here is a treasure this world could not contain.
The house and its landlord
are all pretext and play.

Hands off this house, this talisman.
Don't argue with the landlord;
he's drunk every night.

The dirt and garbage are musk and rose.
The roof and door are music and verse.
In short, whoever finds this house,
is ruler of the world, Solomon of his time.

Look down, Lord, from the roof;
bless us with your glance.

I swear, since seeing Your face,
the whole world is a fraud and fantasy.
The garden is bewildered as to what is leaf
or blossom. The distracted birds
can't distinguish the birdseed from the snare.

A house of love with no limits,
a presence more beautiful than venus or the moon,
a beauty whose image fills the mirror of the heart.

Zulaikha's female friends,
beside themselves in Joseph's presence, sliced their wrists.
Maybe a curl of his hair brushed their hearts.

Come in. The Beloved is here. We are all drunk.
No one notices who enters or leaves.
Don't sit outside the door in the dark, wondering.

Those drunk with God,
even if they are a thousand, live as One.
But drunk with lust, even one is double.

Enter the thicket of lions unafraid of any wounds.
The shadows you fear are just a child's fantasy.

There is no wound and nothing to be wounded;
all is mercy and love.

But you build up thought
like a massive wooden door.
Set fire to the wood.
Silence the noise of the heart.
Hold your harmful tongue.

Elegy for Sana'i

I heard someone say: Master Sana'i is dead.
The death of such a master is no small thing.
He was not some straw pushed by the wind;
he was not water that froze in winter;
he was not a comb that broke in the hair;
he was not a seed swallowed by the earth.
He was a treasure of gold in this dustpit,
because he valued the whole world at a single barleycorn.
The earthly frame he tossed to earth.
Soul and reason he raised aloft.
How strangely the elixir blends with the dregs,
until it settles out within the flask.
A second soul which most humans never know,
I swear by God, he gave to his Beloved.
On a journey, it sometimes happens, my friend,
that a man of Merv or Rayy, a Roman or a Kurd,
travel together before each reaches home.
Should a mature one be the companion of youths?
Be silent as a compass, the King
has erased your name from the book of speech.

The Inner Garment of Love

A soul which is not clothed
with the inner garment of Love
should be ashamed of its existence.

Be drunk with Love,
for Love is all that exists.
Where is intimacy found
if not in the give and take of Love.

If they ask what Love is,
say: the sacrifice of will.
If you have not left your will behind,
you have no will at all.

The lover is a king of kings
with both worlds beneath him;
and a king does not regard
what lies at his feet.

Only Love and the lover
can resurrect beyond time.
Give your heart to this;
the rest is second-hand.

How long will you embrace
a lifeless beloved?

Embrace that entity
to which nothing can cling.

What sprouts up every spring
will wither by autumn,
but the rose garden of Love
is always green.

Both the rose and the thorn
appear together in spring,
and the wine of the grape
is not without its headaches.

Don't be an impatient
bystander on this path —
by God there's no death
worse than expectation.

Set your heart on hard cash
if you are not counterfeit,
and listen to this advice
if you are not a slave:

Don't falter on the horse
of the body; go more lightly on foot.
God gives wings to those
who are not content to ride an ass.

Let go of your worries
and be completely clear-hearted,
like the face of a mirror
that contains no images.

When it is empty of forms,
all forms are contained in it.
No face would be ashamed
to be so clear.

If you want a clear mirror,
behold yourself
and see the shameless truth
which the mirror reflects.

If metal can be polished
to a mirror-like finish,
what polishing might the mirror
of the heart require?

Between the mirror and the heart
is this single difference:
the heart conceals secrets,
while the mirror does not.

This Body is a Rose

*E*ach form you see has its unseen archetype.
If the form is transient, its essence is eternal.
If you have known beauty in a face
or wisdom in a word,
let this counsel your heart:
what perishes is not real.

Since the springhead is timeless,
its branches refresh.
Since neither can cease,
what is the cause of your sorrow?

Think of the soul as source
and created things as springs.
While the source exists,
the springs continually flow.

Empty your head of grief
and drink from the stream.
Don't think of it failing—
this water is endless.

From the moment you came into the manifest world,
a ladder was offered for your escape.
From mineral substance you became a living plant,
and later a roving animal. Is this a secret?

Afterwards, as a human being,
you developed reason, consciousness, faith.
See how this body has risen from the dust like a rose?

When you have surpassed the human state,
your angelic nature will unfold
in a world beyond this world.
Surpass the angels then and enter the Sea.

Your drop will merge with a hundred Seas of Oman.
Let go of him you called "son,"
and say "One" with your life.
Although your body has aged,
your soul has become young.

Empty the Glass of Your Desire

Join yourself to friends
and know the joy of the soul.
Enter the neighborhood of ruin
with those who drink to the dregs.

Empty the glass of your desire
so that you won't be disgraced.
Stop looking for something out there
and begin seeing within.

Open your arms if you want an embrace.
Break the earthen idols and release the radiance.
Why get involved with a hag like this world?
You know what it will cost.

And three pitiful meals a day
is all that weapons and violence can earn.
At night when the Beloved comes
will you be nodding on opium?

If you close your mouth to food,
you can know a sweeter taste.
Our Host is no tyrant. We gather in a circle.
Sit down with us beyond the wheel of time.

Here is the deal: give one life
and receive a hundred.

Stop growling like dogs,
and know the shepherd's care.

You keep complaining about others
and all they owe you?
Well, forget about them;
just be in His presence.

When the earth is this wide,
why are you asleep in a prison?
Think of nothing but the source of thought.
Feed the soul; let the body fast.

Avoid knotted ideas;
untie yourself in a higher world.
Limit your talk
for the sake of timeless communion.

Abandon life and the world,
and find the life *of* the world.

To Know the Moon and the Sea

At the break of dawn a single moon appeared,
descended from the sky, and gazed at me.

Like a falcon swooping in for the catch,
it snatched me up and soared across the sky.
When I looked at myself, I saw myself no more,
because by grace my body had become fine.

I made a journey of the soul accompanied by the moon,
until the secret of time was totally revealed.
Heaven's nine spheres were in that moon.
The vessel of my being had vanished in that sea.

Waves rose on the ocean. Intelligence ascended
and sounded its call. So it happened; so it was.
The sea began to foam and every bit of froth
took shape and was bodied forth.

Then each spindrift body kissed by that sea
immediately melted into spirit.
Without the power of a Shams, the Truth of Tabriz,
one could neither behold the moon nor become the sea.

A Night for Departure

O lovers, lovers, it is time
to set out from the world.
I hear a drum in my soul's ear
coming from the depths of the stars.

Our camel driver is at work;
the caravan is being readied.
He asks that we forgive him
for the disturbance he has caused us,
He asks why we travelers are asleep.

Everywhere the murmur of departure;
the stars, like candles
thrust at us from behind blue veils,
and as if to make the invisible more plain,
a wondrous people have come forth.

Beneath this water wheel of stars
your sleep has been heavy.
Observe that heaviness and beware...
for life is fragile and quick.

Heart, aim yourself at Love!
Friend, discover the Friend!
Watchman, wake up!
You're not here to sleep.

Noise and action on every side,
fires and torches, tonight
this pregnant world gives birth to eternity.
Lifeless clay is living heart.
The inept become aware.

What draws you now
will lead you further,
and as it draws you to Itself,
what pleasure your suffering becomes.

Its fires are like water.
Don't let your face be disturbed.
To be present in the soul is Its work,
and to break your vows.
By Its complex art these atoms
are trembling in their hearts.

O vain puppet, proclaiming
your importance from a hole,
how long will you leap?
Humble yourself,
or they will destroy you.
You have tended seeds of deceit
and practiced contempt.
O pimp, the eternal Truth
was cheapened in your hands!
O ass, covered with dirt
and greedy for mere straw.

There is another within
by whom these eyes sparkle.
If water scalds, it is from the fire;
let this be understood.

I have no stone in my hand,
no quarrel with anyone.
I rebuke no man, but possess
the sweetness of the rose garden.

My eye is from that Source,
from another universe.
One world on this side, another on that,
as I sit on the threshold.
On the threshold are they alone
whose language is silence.
Enough has been uttered;
say no more; hold back the tongue.

The Color of Purity

Inside myself I breathe
the fragrance of the Friend.

In the garden last night
an urge ran through my head;
a sun shone out of my eyes;
an inner river began to flow.

Lips became laughing roses
without the thorns of existence,
safe from the sword of decay.

The trees and plants in the meadow,
which to normal eyes looked fixed and still,
seemed to dance.
When our tall Cypress appeared,
the garden lost itself entirely,
and the plane tree clapped its hands.

A face of fire, a burning wine,
a blazing love, all happy together,
and the self, overwhelmed, screaming,
"Let me out of here."

In the world of Unity
there's no room for number.
But out of necessity number exists
in the worlds of five and four.

[80]

You can count a hundred thousand
sweet apples in your hands.
If you wish to make them one,
crush them all together!

Without thinking of the letters,
listen to the language of the heart.
The color of purity
belongs to the creative Source.
Where the Sun of Tabriz sits,
my verses line up like willing slaves.

Words of 'Ali when he refused
to kill an opponent who spat in his face

For God's sake, for Reality
whose slave I am, I wield this sword.
The body does not command me,
nor does the lion of craving
overcome the lion of God.
Like a sword wielded by the sun,
I embody these words in war:
Thou didst not throw when thou threwest.
I've dropped the baggage of self.
That which is not God is nothing.
God is the sun, and I am a shadow.
Jewelled with the pearls of Union,
my sword bring life in battle, not death.
Blood will not dull my shining sword;
nor will the wind blow my sky away.
I am not chaff but a mountain of patience.
What fierce wind could lift a mountain?
What the wind blows away is trash,
and winds blow from every side—
the winds of anger, lust, and greed
carry away those who do not keep
the times of prayer. I am a mountain,
and my being is His building.
If I am tossed like a straw,
it is His wind that moves me.
Only His wind stirs my desires.
My Captain is love of the One.

Anger is a king over kings,
but anger, once bridled, may serve.
A gentle sword struck the neck of anger.
God's anger came on like mercy.

My roof in ruins; I drown in light.
Though called "the father of dust,"
I have grown like a garden.
And so I must put down my sword,
that my name might be *He loves for God's sake,*
that my desire may be *He hates for God's sake,*
that my generosity might be *He gives for God's sake.*
My stinginess is for God, as are my gifts.
I belong to God, not to anyone else;
and what I do is not a show,
not imagined, not thought up, but seen.
Set free from effort and searching,
I have tied my sleeve to the cuff of God—
if I am flying, I see where I fly;
if I am whirling, I know the axis on which I turn;
if I am dragging a burden, I know to where.
I am the moon, and the sun is in front of me.
I cannot tell the people more than this.
Can the river contain the Sea?

Mathnawi, I, 3787-3810

The Grave is a Veil

On that fatal day when my casket rolls along,
don't think my heart is in this world.
Don't cry, don't wail in anguish;
don't fall into a hole the demons have dug.
That surely would be sad.

When you see my procession, don't say I'm gone.
It will be my reunion.
As you lower me into the grave, don't say, "So long."
The grave is a veil before the gathering of paradise.

When you see that lowering down,
think of a rising.

What harm is in the setting moon or sun?
What seems a setting to you is a dawning.

Though it may seem a prison,
this vault releases the soul.
Unless a seed enters the earth, it doesn't grow.
Why are you doubting this human seed?
Unless the bucket goes down,
it won't come up full.
Why should the Joseph of the Spirit resent the well?

Close your mouth here and open it beyond,
and in the nowhere, air will be your song.

That Which Has No Clue

At the last you vanished, gone to the Unseen.

Strange the path you took out of this world.
Strange how your beating wings demolished the cage,
and you flew away to the world of the soul.

You were some old woman's favorite falcon,
but when you heard the falcon drum,
you escaped to the placeless.

You were a drunken nightingale among owls,
but when the scent of the rose-garden reached you,
you were gone.

The bitter wine you drank with us left its headache,
but at last you entered a timeless tavern.
Like an arrow you went straight for the target of bliss,
straight to the mark like an arrow from a bow.

Like a ghoul, the world tried to deceive you
with its false clues, but you refused the clues,
and went straight to that which had no clue.

Now that you are the sun, what good is a crown?
And how do you tie your belt,
now that you've vanished from the middle?

Heart, what a rare bird you are,
that in your yearning for heaven's attention,
you flew to the spear-point like a shield!

The rose flees autumn,
but what a foolhardy rose you are,
seeking the autumn wind.

You were rain from another world
that fell on this dusty earth.
You ran in all directions
and escaped down the gutter.

Be silent. Be free
of the pain of speech.
Don't sleep, since you took refuge
with so loving a Friend.

Appendix:
A Note on the Thirteenth Century.

Jeláluddin Rúmí was born in 1207 in the city of Balkh in the Persian province of Khorasan, in what is present day Afghanistan. He was from a distinguished family which traced itself back to Abú Bakr, the first caliph of Islam. His father, Bahá'uddin, was a professor of religion, one of the most eminent in that great city. Despite their comfortable situation, Baha'uddin decided to uproot his family and seek a new home somewhere to the south, for these were the days of Chengiz Khan, when much of central Asia and the world was being overrun by the Mongol hordes. The step was well taken, because Balkh would eventually be sacked and most of its inhabitants slaughtered.

    The family first traveled to Nishapur where they were met by the great poet Fariduddin 'Attar, who presented the young Jelál with a copy of his *Asrár-náma (Book of Mysteries)* and said: "This child is destined to set the hearts of many aflame." The family would travel to Baghdad, Mecca, and Damascus before finally settling in Konya (Iconium), capital of the Seljuk Empire, a stable and peaceful haven in those times. In Konya Bahá'uddin accepted an important teaching position, which his son would inherit, and this ancient city on the high Anatolian plain would become the lifelong home of Jeláluddin and his descendants for generations to come.

    The thirteenth century was a time of fruition and

destruction, of decadence and rebirth. Peter of Aragon had approved the burning of heretics in 1197, and Pope Innocent III staged a twenty-year campaign of extermination against the Cathari (1209-1229), a heretical sect that emphasized poverty and simplicity. Whole cities were slaughtered if even half the population was suspected of being associated with the sect. It was around this time that Pope Innocent IV sanctioned the torture of heretics and the distribution of their property among lay officials.

While the Inquisition was beginning in Europe, and Chengiz Khan was ravaging much of the Eastern lands, many of the greatest spiritual personalities of the last two thousand years were planting seeds that would be harvested for centuries to come. The twelfth century saw the establishment of scholasticism in Europe, with Paris and Oxford becoming famed for theology. It was at this time that Albertus Magnus brought so much through his Arabian commentaries, and his student, Thomas Aquinas (1225-1274), would be responsible for introducing many Neoplatonist ideas into Christianity. Saint Dominic founded an order based on apostolic poverty in 1216, and Saint Francis is known to have been conversing with the Sultan of Egypt in 1219. Meister Eckhart and Johannes Tauler, both Dominicans, were developing a Celtic-Germanic mysticism that had much in common with the metaphysics of Spain's Ibn 'Arabi, who was nearly their contemporary.

This same period produced many of the greatest spiritual and literary figures of Islamic culture since the days of the Prophet. Late in the twelfth century Al-Ghazzálli had succeeded in integrating the mystical ideas of Sufism with orthodox theology, and thereby bringing these ideas more into the mainstream. In Persia, Suhrawardi Maqtu'l (1153-1191) had synthesized a grand theosophy of illumination from Islamic and ancient Persian sources, incorporating the wisdom of centuries if not millennia. In this century, too, Sana'i wrote *Hadiqat al-haqiqa (The Orchard of Truth)*, which became the model for much of the didactic mystical poetry that followed, including Rumi's *Mathnáwi*. The heights of Islamic metaphysical speculation were reached by Ibn 'Arabi (1165-1240), known as "the Pole of Knowledge." It was he who wrote: "God becomes the mirror in which the spiritual man contemplates his own reality and in turn becomes the mirror in which God contemplates His names and qualities." Sadruddin Qonawí (d.1274), his disciple and foremost interpreter, emigrated to Konya and was closely associated with Mevlána.

In addition to Attár, Ibn al-Farid (d.1235), another great poet of mystical love, wrote his delicate and refined verses in Egypt. While in Turkey, Yunus Emre sang his songs of mystical love in the Turkish vernacular. Another immigrant from Khorasan at this time was the great and enigmatic Hadji Bektash (1247-1338), founder of an important dervish order. Meanwhile, Mu'inuddin Chisti arrived in Delhi just fourteen years before Mevlána's birth. He and his successors were responsible for the introduction of Islam into India through a lively and devotional Sufism that gained great popularity among the people.

In briefest outline these are some of the personalities that helped to make the thirteenth century an unrivaled time for mystical inspiration.

Sources of Translations

[F] Furuzunfar, Badi-uz-Zaman. *Kulliyat-e Shams*, Tehran: 1966.
[M] Nicholson, R.A. *The Mathnáwi of Jalaluddin Rumi*. London, 1925-40.
    Including Persian text, translation, and commentary.
[D] *Selected Poems from the Divani Shamsi Tabriz*. Cambridge, 1898. A critical
    edition including Persian text.

Classic Sufi literature available from Threshold:

Rumi:
Open Secret, Versions of Rumi $9
Translated by John Moyne, Coleman Barks
Unseen Rain, Quatrains $9
Translated by John Moyne, Coleman Barks
This Longing, Poetry & Letters $9
Translated by Coleman Barks, John Moyne
Feeling The Shoulder of the Lion, Poetry & Teaching Stories $9
Translated by Coleman Barks
Rumi: Daylight, A Daybook of Spiritual Guidance $19
Translated by Camille & Kabir Helminski
Love is a Stranger, Selected Lyric Poetry $9
Translated by Kabir Edmund Helminski

Other Sufi Poetry:
The Drop That Became The Sea, Yunus Emre $8
Translated by Kabir Helminski, Refik Algan
Happiness Without Death, Assad Ali $9
Translated by Helminski, Shihabi
Doorkeeper of the Heart, Versions of Rabi'a $8
Versions by Charles Upton

Other Books on Sufism:
The Most Beautiful Names $11
Shaikh Tosun Bayrak
Love is the Wine, Talks of a Sufi Master $9
Shaikh Muzaffer Ozak
What the Seeker Needs, Writings of Ibn 'Arabi $10
Translated by Bayrak & Harris
Awakened Dreams, Raji's Journeys with the Mirror Dede $13
Ahmet Hilmi, translated by Algan & C. Helminski
Inspirations on the Path of Blame $13
Shaikh Badruddin of Simawna, Translated by Bayrak

Send payment plus $3 for 1st book, $.50 each additional to:
Threshold Books, RD 4, Box 600, Putney, VT 05346
Order by phone (credit cards accepted): (802) 257-2779